All Scripture references taken from the KJV of the Holy Bible, unless otherwise indicated.

The Fear of Money by Dr. Marlene Miles

Freshwater Press 2025

Freshwaterpress9@gmail.com

ISBN: 978-1-967860-16-6

Paperback Version

Table of Contents

The Fear of Money

Freshwater

Nobody Asked Jesus for Money

Nobody in the Bible asked Jesus for money.

This may be why many say that it is not good, or even sinful to talk about money.

And having food and raiment let us be therewith content. **But they that will be rich fall into temptation and a snare, and *into* many foolish and hurtful lusts, which drown men in destruction and perdition.** For the love of money is the root of all evil: which while some coveted after, they have erred from the faith, and pierced themselves through with many sorrows. But thou, O man of God, flee these things; and follow after righteousness, godliness, faith, love, patience, meekness. Fight the good fight of faith, lay hold on eternal life, whereunto thou art also called, and hast professed a good profession before many witnesses. (1 Timothy 6:8-12)

Now, in the Old Testament there were instances of people needing money, but in the New Testament, no one came to Jesus and said, Lord, give me money or I need money.

Many think that Christians shouldn't talk about money; it's a bad word. Jesus talked about money about 250 times in the New Testament. 11 of his 39 parables were about money. Yes, there are a lot of warnings, and we will see why later.

The only thing talked about in the Bible; the whole bible more than money was **food**. There are about 2500 Bible verses about money. So #1 is Food. #2 is Money.

Some people are afraid of money, among many other reasons why people may shun money and wealth is that a person may not feel worthy of having money or having a lot of money.

They say money burns a hole in some people's pockets as to why some people don't have money or can't seem to keep it. There are spiritual influences that will promote the spending of or the using up money. Greed. Pride. Competition. Cheating, as in having a secret or double life--, so liars will spend extra money. Folks with no administrative skill in money management may burn through money. Spoiled and entitled people don't value money. People with an unsanctioned Mercy gift may blow through money. Their Mercy gift is not tempered, by the

Holy Spirit and is therefore, over the top. Which leads us into the next group.

Some feel guilty because others don't have, when they have. Some want to save the world. Yes, save the world, the part of the world that you are called to. Jesus came to save the whole world, but we are not Jesus. But save the part of the world that you are called to.

Parents teach kids to share with their siblings. Is that forever? Is your wallet forever attached to your siblings. So, you get educated and get a great job, but your sibling does nothing. They don't even work: is your wallet tied to your siblings for your entire life? There can be deep family money altars that may be the downfall of a person or the entire family. We are taught to help bring one another up, but one sinner can destroy a lot of good. You are not the spouse of your sibling, that is legally impossible and spiritually criminal.

Yes, we are our brother's keeper, but who is your brother? Jesus said it is he who does the will of God. So, while one is diligent and working to be successful and the other, or others are not, every time you mix your money in with theirs you share in their issues as much or more than they share in your success. Family money altars are attended to and family idols are worshipped every time you pay homage to the family money altar with your own money, even if you are serving Christ.

What of the man who finds a wife and leaves and cleaves. Cleave is an interesting word. It is cutting, dividing, separating. We know there is a knife in the kitchen set called a cleaver. But it also means to adhere to and stick to. This word means both things. What is the man cleaving? He is cutting off apron strings and umbilical cords of the family of birth to start his own family.

There are some people who only want to make so much because their parents or grandparents told them to stay at C level, which is average--, don't rock the boat in order to avoid problems. The timid or fearful warn their son or daughter of the story of the man drives his luxury car to work and gets fired because his boss is jealous of the man's new car.

Some are still suffering under slave mentality where they think they shouldn't have anything. This could have been passed on through generations or it could be recent familial structure where one or more believe they are to carry the family while others enjoy the fruits of that person's toil. *Jr. is doing well, so he must help the entire family.*

Some need a job, for example, but can only make so much at whatever job they choose, or they lose their disability, by working so many hours. proving they are not disabled, or they lose other benefits. If you don't know what I'm talking about, then I'm not talking to you. IYKYK.

If you know what I'm talking about, then you know.

Some don't want money because of low self-esteem, they don't think they deserve money or don't deserve much money. Some have no self-esteem.

Someone recently said to me, "More money, more problems." Sadly, if that's their mantra then they will get what they say.

Some don't want money because they think it's a problem or will bring problems. Depends on where you got the money. Money from God makes rich and He adds no sorrow. Money not from God, money from the dark kingdom will bring all kinds of sorrow and affliction.

Devil Steals

Spiritually why do you think the enemy messes with people's money so much unless it is okay or needful to have money. Nearly 40 million people in the US live in poverty. Why do you think they don't have enough?

I'd say spiritual things that need to be sorted out because the devil steals from folks. Why would the devil take money from this many folks? If money is a bad thing, then why would the devil take it from people? Wouldn't he want them to keep the *bad* thing?

It's to control them. Have power over them. Have what should be theirs. The devil wants it, reroutes it, uses it…

Stockpiles it and uses it for his dark agenda in his dark kingdom. It takes money to run a kingdom—good or evil, it takes money, which of course, is a power.

Some are afraid of money and may not pursue spiritually to get it for many reasons. The main reason is lack of awareness that the problem is spiritual. Another reason they may not pursue is lack of knowledge as to how to. Then there is the problem of having enough anointing; if a person is not spiritual, they just aren't. So now the problem becomes if deliverance is needed, finding either how to self-deliver or they may have a problem finding a real deliverance minister.

The last time I had it. Every time I get it. These are evil imaginations that need to be cast down in the Name of Jesus.

Some people think that money is a burden to some. It can be, but the blessings of the Lord make rich and He adds no sorrow with it. People have adverse feelings and reactions to money because of demonic trickery and past history. The devil can add sorrow to anything to make you not like it, like putting hot sauce on a thumb to get your toddler from putting it in his mouth. Putting a bad taste in your mouth regarding money, or give a person a bad memory regarding money when that is not what God intended at all is an emotional trauma that the devil likes to inflict upon people.

As a Christian, it is your decision or problem if you decide to embrace this trauma and hold on to it and let it become a stronghold in your life. This is a soul prosperity issue.

Beloved I pray above all things that you would prosper and be in health, even as your soul prospers. (3 John 2)

Some don't want to handle money. Some hate math and do not want to involve themselves in it.

Some are indoctrinated or brainwashed by the enemy to hate money. Yet, I'm not sure how any of us can do our purpose without money.

However, overly loving money is a demonic construct. Woe to him that would be rich.

Hating money, fearing money is also a demonic construct. Let your moderation be shown. From Proverbs 30, Solomon asked the Lord to have enough that he would not steal.

Remove far from me vanity and lies: give me neither poverty nor riches; feed me with food convenient for me:

Lest I be full, and deny thee, and say, Who is the Lord? or lest I be poor, and steal, and take the name of my God in vain, (Proverbs 30:8-9)

Some people are afraid of money and success. God gives them a good idea, a God idea; they give it away. They don't want to do it. They are afraid to do it. They don't know how to even start doing it, or can't even believe it is for them. But it may make their life very prosperous and make their purpose possible, in the Name of Jesus.

People give their money away. They give away the food in their house, they give the shirt off their own back. Perhaps they feel very abundant and want to share. Maybe their mercy gift is over the top. Perhaps they don't feel worthy. Perhaps they were trained that way or influenced by spirits from the dark kingdom without even realizing it. Such as a *people pleasing spirit* and they want to people to like them.

It is up to us as individuals if that is something that we are doing to know why we are doing it. If it is of God, well

Amen, carry on. If not, then we seek deliverance. Just the Word of Truth can deliver a person. One can receive self-deliverance, it doesn't have to be a dramatic visit to a deliverance minister.

Perhaps they have a deep gift of helps and they love helping people. Some people are givers. Their job may be to heap money and give it to whomever God says for them to give it to.

Notice how very rich people don't seem to want to give money until they get up in age, then all of a sudden, they not only want to give it all away, but they also want to announce that they are giving it all away. Yet, you could meet a rich person and even tell them your entire idea, or your entire story, your entire plight and they could just look at you as if something is wrong with you and tell you, No.. Or, they could just say, No before you spill all the details of your life. Still, they are adept at saying, No and not giving away or lending very much or anything at all. But some years later, they are now announcing that they are giving it all away or leaving it all to their cat or dog.

Some people see money as a burden: I want to keep friends. If I have more money than they do, they will be jealous of me, or hate me. I have more than they do and I want to keep my friends. Folks, some will hate you if you have a lot of money and others will hate you if you are broke. So which state would be more comfortable for you, since you might be hated anyway? Many times it is not money or lack of money, although you may think it is. Many times the hate is because you are Christian, and they are not. Sometimes folks just don't like the Spirit in you especially if that Spirit doesn't match their *spirit* or *spirits*.

Jesus said, Marvel not if they hate you,
for they hated Me first.
Marvel not, my brethren, if the world
hate you (1 John 3:13)

Don't hold back who you are and what you're made of so you can be average or normal or so you don't outshine your friends, family, or spouse. Be the you God created you to be. Dumbing yourself down will make you miserable and not more loved. Making yourself smaller or slower will not make people love you. Why do I say that?

Because you will be miserable when you are not your authentic God-created self. And when you are miserable, you will make others miserable, and you will attract misery. Therefore, being broke when God has wealth for you to receive, have, manage, use, and bless others with is foolish and will not make you have more friends.

As for me, I noticed that I had more "friends" when I was a certain size.

19

When I lost weight and was more svelte--, no friends. Were those people really friends?

Some folks don't want money because they are worrying about what people will think of them. If you think having too much money is going to be a problem for you, ask yourself, *Did God tell you to broadcast your financials?* Then shut up about how much money you have. Use money well, do good things with it, but don't broadcast it.

Some don't want money because they don't want to be used. That includes friends, relatives, and even strangers. *Women only date me because of my money.* Or, *Men only date me because of my money.*

If you are a soul who is not called to steward over money, that's between you and God, but I believe most are. Some have made a vow of poverty which to me only looks as though they are saying, let someone else handle the details. Those who take these "vows" are still eating and have a place to live. They have the necessities of life, but someone else is handling the money part of things.

People who are afraid of math and may have a **fear** of numbers or math may shun money. But God didn't give us **a** *spirit of fear*, but one of love power and of a sound mind. **A** *spirit of fear?* Is there is more than one? If that were not so, the passage would have read, **the** *spirit of fear*. Therefore, getting rid of fear may take a lot of work.

Even though people didn't approach Jesus with brazen requests for money, even though people don't think Christians should talk about it, we still need money. It is okay to ask the Father for anything in the Name of Jesus.

And in that day ye shall ask me nothing. Verily, verily, I say unto you, Whatsoever ye shall ask the Father in my name, he will give *it* you (John 16:23)

Jesus Gave Wealth

Early in the morning, Jesus stood on the shore, but the disciples did not realize that it was Jesus.

He called out to them, "Friends, haven't you any fish?"

"No," they answered.

He said, "Throw your net on the right side of the boat and you will find some." When they did, they were unable to haul the net in because of the large number of fish.

Then the disciple whom Jesus loved said to Peter, "It is the Lord!" As soon as Simon Peter heard him say, "It is the Lord," he wrapped his outer garment around him (for he had taken it off) and jumped into the water. The other disciples followed in the boat, towing the net full of fish, for they were not far from shore, about a hundred yards. When they landed, they saw a fire of burning coals there with fish on it, and some bread.

Jesus said to them, "Bring some of the fish you have just caught." So Simon Peter climbed back into the boat and dragged the net ashore. It was full of large fish, but even with so many the net was not torn. (John 21:4-11)

Jesus is Lord of the Harvest, so there should be no mystery as to why the catch was so large.

Jesus can get wealth to you without any loss, destruction, drama or trauma. Why would He do that? Because you need it and because it is yours. Because He came to redeem mankind from poverty. Because He can. It is yours. Because you have been sent to Earth on a mission and missions require finances. Those finances have already been apportioned to you, so it would be wrong to not at least look for it, expect it, take stewardship over it, use it, and go get it if it has been stolen from you. Money is a weapon. If a weapon has been stolen from you, you need to go get it back before it is used against you or against someone else.

Jesus came that you would have an abundant life. Not having enough, being in lack is very stressful; Jesus came to remedy that for mankind.

> The thief comes to steal, kill, and to destroy. (John 10:10)

The fishermen who would be Jesus' future Disciples did not ask Jesus for money or wealth or a significant catch, and they didn't even know He could do this. In addition, we know that at least twice Jesus fed great multitudes of people. These immediate and needful blessings are because of Jesus being the Lord of the Harvest, and does not withhold blessings from people. But there was no line where people came around and had money placed in their hands.

Jesus Calls His First Disciples

One day as Jesus was standing by the Lake of Gennesaret, the people were crowding around him and listening to the word of God. He saw at the water's edge two boats, left there by the fishermen, who were washing their nets. He got into one of the boats, the one belonging to Simon, and asked him to put out a little from shore. Then he sat down and taught the people from the boat.

When he had finished speaking, he said to Simon, "Put out into deep water, and let down the nets for a catch."

Simon answered, "Master, we've worked hard all night and haven't caught anything. But because you say so, I will let down the nets."

When they had done so, they caught such a large number of fish that their nets began to break. So they signaled their partners in the other boat to come and help them, and they came and filled both boats so full that they began to sink.

When Simon Peter saw this, he fell at Jesus' knees and said, "Go away from me, Lord; I am a sinful man!" For he and all his companions were astonished at the catch of fish they had taken, and so were James and John, the sons of Zebedee, Simon's partners.

Then Jesus said to Simon, "Don't be afraid; from now on you will fish for people." So they pulled their boats up on shore, left everything and followed him. (Luke 5:1-11)

The Lord can send you so much that there won't even be enough room to receive it. These are <u>blessings</u> from God, not curses. Money from God is not a curse, it is a blessing, (Malachi 3). You're not worried about having too much, are you?

Of note, Jesus got the attention of these men with power and that power was wealth because they would sell the fish to make money. Jesus' first miracle is said to have been turning water into wine, but this great catch where Jesus first drew Disciples happened before the wedding feast. So, are we to surmise that the great catch of fish was not a miracle? Is this then an everyday occurrence for us? Do we run the risk of being wildly successful daily?

1. Lord, let it be, amen.

(But I still feel that this was a miracle.)

Fear Repels Money

Fear repels money. Any fear. Any kind of fear. Fear of anything, but especially the fear of money will put up a wall between you and money so it will not come to you. The thief is busy blocking you from getting blessings from God, don't you be complicit in helping him keep you in lack, or poor and in poverty. A most heartbreaking reason not to reach destiny is to not be able to finance it, when the money was available for you all along. As heart breaking would be not being married or happily married, or have a home or children or be able to educate your children because of lack of finances, when God is trying to give you money, but the devil has put up barriers and obstacles, but you may have put up strongholds or allowed strongholds o remain without doing any spiritual warfare to tear them down.

Fear is a very powerful stronghold. Fear is the opposite of Love. Fear, not hate is the opposite of Love. The gifts of God work by Love. Love is a power. The blessings of the Lord come to those who God calls His own. Those who God calls *His* look like God, act like God, talk like God. They love. If you don't have love, the New Testament says, then you are nothing. I'd like to add that a person without love may also have nothing. Sin repels wealth from God. The works of the flesh repel money coming to you.

Grumpy, angry, irritated, petty people, unless they are mooching off of someone else, often have very little to nothing. Anger especially pushes people, things, and blessings away from you. It is said that there is a spirit that rejoices every time a person goes into anger, even over the smallest and pettiest things because they know that day that person will not receive anything from the Lord. So, their job is to torment and egg a person on until they erupt in anger--, even anger in their heart. Even if they never explode and yell at anyone or anything worse. By connecting with anger, they have blocked their blessing and most often repelling it. Well, do that day after day and soon the blessing stream will dry up, if there was ever one.

Thirty-Seven Miracles

Jesus' two fishing boat miracles were financial, ultimately. However, Jesus performed 37 miracles. Of those miracles who asked Jesus for money?

Old Testament widows needed money and were blessed through prophets of God.

The poor you have with you always. More than 40% of the world's population is poor or live in poverty. Yet, in the Bible, no one directly asked Jesus for money. The Gospels do not mention anyone specifically asking Him for money.

People came to Jesus for healing. Blind men, lepers, the woman with the issue of blood all came for healing. They came to Him to ask forgiveness of sins, such as the paralyzed man who had been lowered through the roof by his friends.

They asked Him for deliverance from oppressing and tormenting demons. They sought Jesus for Wisdom or guidance on issues such as eternal life. Wisdom was accessed when Jesus judged the issue of the woman caught in adultery.

Money wealth, sufficiency or supply is a result of deliverance because a battle has been fought, won, and spoils are received. So, asking for the spiritual thing and by gaining spiritually, the natural thing just comes to you. This begs the question then, if you didn't need spiritual deliverance, would the blessing automatically have come to you?

Yes. Because there would have been no spiritual interference.

And, yes because the answers to our prayers from God are Yes, and Amen. But now the path is cleared and the blessings that God has released are able to get to you.

The closest case involving money might be the tribute tax issue (Matthew 22:15–22), where Jesus is asked about paying taxes to Caesar. This is not a personal request for money, but a political trap. No one asked for money for personal use from Jesus.

Judas Iscariot, who handled the money bag for the Disciples, probably had some comfort in handling finances, or at least acted as if he did.

No one is recorded as asking Jesus directly for money in the Bible, unless you count needing to pay the tax to

Ceasar which they did by retrieving a coin from a fish's mouth.

Instead, people went to Jesus for healing, truth, mercy, and transformation—not material wealth. Unlike in the Old Testament when the two different widow women needed money to remedy their respective situations. These are two different stories with two different prophets.

When Jesus did address money, it was often to warn about its dangers or to shift focus toward eternal things and not physical and temporal things. (like in the story of the rich young ruler or the parable of the rich fool).

In the Gospels, very few rich people are recorded as coming to Jesus directly—and even fewer spoke to Him about eternal life or spiritual matters. Could that be because they had money, so they already had the *god* they wanted to worship?

People who were vexed and tormented, and halt, and lame, and blind, asked for deliverance from those maladies, and not for money. They had the Wisdom to know what was wrong with them was a spiritual problem, and they asked a spiritual person for a spiritual correction. (Matthew 19:16–22, Mark 10:17–22, Luke 18:18–23.)

Money is spiritual, but it is not what is needed instead of the casting out of a demon. And it is not the typical pathway of casting out a demon, else all rich people would be demon less.

Uh--.

The rich man that came to Jesus asked, "What must I do to inherit eternal life?"

Jesus told him to keep the commandments, then to sell all he had, give to the poor, and follow Him. That was either a lesson to the young man, or Jesus didn't want the kind of money he had to be put in His ministry's treasury. (or both).

That rich young man went away sorrowful, because he had great wealth, that he was very attached to and obviously was not planning to get rid of.

Nicodemus, a wealthy Pharisee and member of the Sanhedrin, (John 3:1–21), came at night to discuss Jesus' teachings. Jesus spoke to him about being "born again" and eternal life. Later, Nicodemus contributed to the ministry of Jesus when he helped by providing expensive spices for Jesus' burial, which clearly showed his wealth (John 19:39),

Joseph of Arimathea (Matthew 27:57–60, John 19:38–42) was a rich man and secret follower of Jesus. This Joseph asked Pilate for Jesus' body and buried Him in his own unused tomb. I Am That I Am: a *Joseph* helped Jesus to come to this Earth realm by being his Earth father, and another Joseph helped Him to be buried. The name Joseph means, *he will add.* Both were destiny helpers facilitating Jesus' purpose for coming to Earth.

Businessmen

Some of Jesus' disciples were involved in business-like trades, particularly fishing and tax collection,

In the Old Testament, David had broke, busted and disgusted men following him. In the New Testament, Jesus had tradesman and businessmen. If money was such a bad thing, wouldn't Jesus have only added the poor to His roster of Disciples instead of getting people with means? The answer is because there is nothing wrong with having money. Not only that, Jesus talked to people who had money, dealt with money, knew something about money, **about money**.

But as long as the devil can make people believe that it is, then he will put up barriers to the Gospel going forth that require money. If the super holy people don't have any money, then the Word of God does not go forth. That's right up there with the devil having convinced people that he doesn't exist. But he does exist. And money is needed for ministry.

It's because money is not a bad thing if it is used as the instrument that it is and used properly.

The four Disciples, Peter, Andrew, James, and John were commercial fishermen (Matthew 4:18–22, Luke 5:1–11.) These four were partners in a fishing business on the Sea of Galilee. They owned boats and worked with nets in a commercial operation.

James and John worked with their father Zebedee and had hired servants (Mark 1:20), indicating some type of established business.

Matthew (Levi) was a tax Collector (Matthew 9:9, Luke 5:27–28). He worked for the Roman government collecting taxes, which was a lucrative and despised job, and he likely had become wealthy from the job.

Other Disciples, Philip, Bartholomew, Thomas, Thaddeus, Simon the Zealot, Judas Iscariot—, the Gospels don't tell us much about their former professions.

Judas Iscariot managed the group's money (John 12:6), suggesting he had some financial savvy. If having money was such a bad thing then wouldn't Jesus have told them to get that money out of their hands and follow Him? Why would He have allowed them an amazing catch and then they still followed Him? It was to show us that even an abundant harvest or catch or mega bucks coming in does not compare to the Word of God, the Lord God, Jesus

Christ. It doesn't mean that the families of these men didn't need money and still needed a house to live in and food to eat; it simply meant that God is greater than money. That is why they walked away even from the big catch to become Disciples of Christ. And being commercial fishermen, I suspect they had people working their businesses while they were being discipled. Doesn't the Word say that after Jesus died, some went back to fishing? Well, there had to be a business to go back to, right?

Jesus called people from working-class and marginal professions—practical, hands-on roles—not elite or high-status business positions showing that the Kingdom of God is for every man, any man. Whoever will take up his cross and follow Jesus, not just for those of status and wealth already.

Having money will not make you into a Pharisee if you are not already a pharisee and already have the hardened heart of a Pharisee. Having money won't make you into a criminal, unless you are already a criminal in your heart, and you happen to get this money by criminal means. Having money won't turn you into a heathen, unless you start to worship the money. Money will reveal who you are, though. A person could be a broke pharisee, a pharisee wanna-be. But money wont make you into something that you are not, but it will reveal what you are.

They Needed Money

In the Old Testament there are two examples of people who needed money and divine help to solve their problems. God sent a Prophet to them, letting us know that it is not wrong to ask God for money. Jesus said in the New Testament, ask what you will of the Father and He will give it to you.

The first example is the story of the widow woman and the prophet, Elisha. Through this prophet a miracle was achieved where the widow's oil never ran out (2 Kings 4:1–7). This widow of a prophet cried out to Elisha because her husband had died, and creditors were coming to take her two sons as slaves.

Elisha asked her what she had in the house. She said she had nothing but a jar of oil. Elisha told her to gather empty vessels, and the oil miraculously multiplied until every jar was filled. She sold the oil, paid off her debt, and lived on the rest. Clear case of financial need met by a prophet through a miracle.

On the front end of that story, it was a clear case of the deceased father having to borrow and get into debt with creditors and either not solving the problem of debt or not being able to solve it. This man, before death, didn't clear his debt, be it spiritual, financial, natural or all of those kinds of debt and leaving the problem to his children. Now his children would be enslaved to pay for the father's debt. This could be looked at as the father not realizing that debt is spiritual and didn't handle it spiritually, so it remained for his generations.

The next is the Widow of Zarephath and Elijah and the never-empty jar, (1 Kings 17:8–16). During a famine, Elijah was sent to a poor widow gathering sticks to cook her last meal. She said she had only a handful of flour and a little oil for one final meal with her son. Elijah told her to make him bread first, and God would make sure her flour and oil never ran out. The miracle provided for her, her son, and Elijah throughout the famine.

2. Lord, in the Name of Jesus let there always be enough in my house. Let there always be sufficiency, as You are Jehovah Jireh. As You are El Shaddai, the God of More than Enough.

3. Lord, as Jesus came that we may have life and have it more abundantly, let there always be abundance in my house and in my generations, in the Name of Jesus. Amen.

The story of Naaman the Syrian who had been cured of leprosy by the prophet teaches us some valuable lessons. After being healed, Naaman tried to offer a gift of money to the prophet (5:1–16). Naaman offered money and gifts to Elisha after being healed of leprosy. Elisha refused to accept the payment. Gehazi, Elisha's servant, later ran after Naaman and greedily took the money and was, himself, cursed with leprosy.

When a prophet refuses money, he or she is showing that true prophetic help isn't for sale. (Freely I received, freely I give.) The prophet didn't accept the money because every dollar ain't a good dollar. Gehazi didn't seem to know that as he ran after that money. Goodness and Mercy should be following us. The blessings of the Lord should be overtaking us, that includes success and wealth and money; we are not to be chasing them.

Just as it is uncouth and uncool for a woman to chase a man, since men love to chase, it puts that woman in a masculine energy and the man in a feminine energy. It is perverted. Perversion is never of God. It is the devil that perverts things.

In the same way, we should not chase money, it should chase us as a blessing of the Lord that makes rich and adds no sorrow. The kind of money that is chased is laced with many ungodly things, such as sorrows and afflictions and evil promises that you may not have known that you made when you finally "catch up" to that money. Gehazi learned that, didn't he?

God chasers? Yes. Money chasers? No. Chasing money deifies the money, it exalts it, which is a perversion. This may sound counter to what the world says, and it is. The world says, *Get that money, get that bag.* We are proactive in making a living and doing our purpose that God put us here to do, but money is not the focus and the goal, doing the Will of Him who sent you is the focus. Money is a fruit or a byproduct of that obedience.

After I finished dental school, I had a job that I worked two days a week. Hey, don't despise small beginnings, I had a job. At the end of the pay period, I received a check, and it was for what I thought was a lot of money. I don't know if anyone saw me or not, but I cried silent tears because I didn't know that I would make this much money doing something that I wanted to do. The job was easy in a sense because I wanted to do it. And I got paid for this? This is fantastic. The burden was easy, the yoke was light. Amen. That's a proper relationship with working and money. It should not be working hard to earn a little. It should be working smart or easy and earning a lot.

Kings & Wealth

Kings usually had great wealth, but having great wealth didn't necessarily mean you were a king. In the Bible, many kings sought after material wealth, but that didn't make them all bad.

Jesus is King of kings. Even when He first arrived on Earth He was given a treasury of frankincense, gold, and myrrh. If it was bad to accept wealth wouldn't those gifts have been rejected? It is abundantly clear though that Jesus didn't seek the wealth, the wealth was looking for Him.

So, we too, should have enough, and not be in the ilk of the impoverished.

We shouldn't be looking for or lusting after wealth, it should be looking for us. We are *little k* kings, and we are of a royal priesthood, so we as individuals and collectively should have enough, or more than enough because of whose we are and who we serve. We must be wise with how we use position and authority.

Several kings are associated with seeking material wealth in pursuit of power, some in disobedience,

Solomon was the wealthiest king of all, (1 Kings 3–11, 2 Chronicles 1–9), but he never asked God for money. He asked for the greater thing, *Wisdom*. King Solomon *a*sked God for wisdom, not wealth, but God gave him both.

Solomon became incredibly rich: with an annual income of 25 tons of gold. He built the Temple and his massive palace with gold, cedar, and precious stones. He had imported horses and chariots from Egypt Deut. 17:16–17).

Solomon's downfall started as he accumulated excessive wives, which led him into idolatry. Solomon had a problem with amassing too much stuff. It was as though he was or became a hoarder, hoarding gold? Yes. Hoarding women? Well, that's one way to put it. Whoredoms is spelled with a "w";

Ultimately, Solomon Started well, but his wealth became part of his spiritual downfall.

King Hezekiah showed off his wealth. (2 Kings 20:12–19, Isaiah 39), After his miraculous healing, he showed Babylonian envoys all his treasures: gold, silver, spices, and armory. If Hezikiah had lived in modern times, I am convinced that he would have posted all his riches on social media.

The prophet Isaiah rebuked him, asking, *Who were those men?* Hezekiah said they came from very far away. Isaih wanted to know, *What did you show them?* Hezekiah said I showed them everything. In the prophet's rebuke of the king, Isaiah said, "One day Babylon would carry it all away." There is no need to fear money, but handling money this way these kings, yes, even kings created their own problems. So you can't really blame it on the money, blame it on the man. So, don't fear the money in cases like this, the fear rests in the character or the lack of character, morals, ethics, and godliness of the person handling the money.

Bad Kings

Another king, Ahab who is known for being the worst and most evil king of all coveted Naboth's vineyard, (1 Kings 21). Coveting in the Old Testament is equivalent to idolatry in the New Testament.

Ahab was already a wealthy king, but he wanted one man's vineyard next to his palace. Naboth's vineyard was an inheritance from his own father, and in those days, you never sold anything that is inherited. Ahab wasn't a saved king, so he may not have considered that if you're going to abuse money, God will judge it. That all the more applies to us, since judgment begins in the house of God.

But you should have a Godly fear of God and know and obey the laws of God so you don't have to worry about something happening to you because you handle money.

Ahab coveted the vineyard, and when Naboth refused, Ahab sulked until Jezebel had Naboth killed.

God judged Ahab for this greed and injustice. As well, kings can be female; they are called queens. And we all know what happened to Jezebel in the end.

Ahab had plenty, but coveted more wealth than he had—abused power to get it.

King Rehoboam took wealth and then lost it. (1 Kings 14:25–28). Rehoboam *was* Solomon's son. He was rebellious in his reign, Egypt invaded Jerusalem and took the treasures of the Temple and palace. He replaced the stolen gold shields with bronze ones—a symbolic loss of glory. *This king inherited wealth but lost it due to weak leadership and rebellion.*

Jehoiakim heaped wealth on himself, He built luxury for himself. Money is not for greedy and prideful, but when these traits or spirits are present, money will clearly express it. (Jeremiah 22:13–19). Jehoiakim cared about luxury and self-enrichment while neglecting justice for the poor.

This king was rebuked by Jeremiah for building a palace with forced labor. He used his kingship for selfish gain and was condemned by God.

Foreign kings in the Bible were notoriously bad. They were kings who sought after wealth and once they had it they flaunted it, big time.

The Pharaohs: These Egyptian kings were always linked with gold, wealth, and oppression, especially in the Exodus.

Nebuchadnezzar (Babylon): Took gold vessels from the Temple (Daniel 1:2), built massive wealth and structures. His punishment was severe, he grazed like a wild animal for seven years.

Belshazzar (Babylon): Used Temple vessels to throw a lavish party, was judged that very night (Daniel 5).

In summary, these kings abused wealth, or were brought low by misusing it:

Solomon was given wealth by God but disobeyed God and later descended into idolatry. Hezekiah showed off, was rebuked and later the people he had ruled over were taken into exile. Ahab coveted the wealth of another until Naboth was killed by Ahab's wife, Jezebel.

Rehoboam, was like a rich trust fund kid, inherited wealth from the richest king, ever: Solomon, but lost it through poor leadership and was a cause of a national divide of Israel.

Jehoiakim lived the life at others' expense.

Belshazzar stole temple vessels and had a party. He was killed that same night.

Kings who sought or idolized material wealth often lost spiritual integrity, power, or their entire kingdom. The same is true of any person, a king or otherwise. If you are one who fears that money will destroy you or any part of your life, then pray that the Lord renew a right spirit in you and build your soul's prosperity so you can contain the wealth that the Lord entrusts to you. You have to have enough soul prosperity to manage the wealth you need to do what God sent you here to Earth to do and reach destiny. God will regenerate your spirit, but you are in charge of possessing your soul in sanctification and honor.

Good Kings

So, it is not the wealth that you seek. You seek your purpose. You seek destiny. You seek purpose then define the wealth you need to perform that purpose. Then ask God for it and how it will come to you.

Righteous kings used material wealth in a way to honor God and do the will of God. In the Bible, good kings who had material wealth but used it well, particularly to honor God, led the nation wisely, and blessed others.

You want to save the world? Save the part of the world that you are called to. Don't be surprised to find out that takes finances. Even if your kingdom only has one other person in it. Five people. A hundred. A million--, whoever God has called you to. Use it for that purpose and God will bless you and you will have no problems in having that money. If you are asking God for money and God agrees with how you are going to use it, you will have no problems with having and using that money. Whatever is in a person's heart, the money will enhance it. If you have goodness in your heart, the money will assist you in being good.

David used wealth for worship and toward building the House of God, (1 Chronicles 29, 2 Samuel 8:11, 2 Samuel 24). David accumulated great wealth from military victories, by winning spoils, but dedicated his gains to the Lord. Silver, gold, and bronze from conquered nations were set apart for the Temple, not for David's personal gain.

God didn't allow David to build the Temple, because David was a man of war, but that didn't stop David. David personally gave a massive offering toward the building of the House of God.

> With all my resources I have provided for the temple of my God... Besides, in my devotion... I now give my personal treasures of gold and silver. (1 Chron. 29:2–3)

King David led a public offering for the Temple and inspired the leaders and people to give generously. His attitude was one of humility. It is recorded that he said, "Who am I... that we should be able to give as generously as this? Everything comes from You." (1 Chron. 29:14). David Used wealth to glorify God, not himself. David led by example in sacrificial giving.

King Jehoshaphat enjoyed prosperity with Godly reform while he ruled, (2 Chronicles 17–20). Jehoshaphat became wealthy and powerful through God's favor (2 Chron. 17:5). He used his position and resources to accomplish great things for his people and kingdom.

Education was important to this king, so he sent teachers of the Law throughout Judah (17:7–9). He strengthened defense and infrastructure wisely. He sought prophetic and wise, Godly counsel before battles (2 Chron. 20).

King Jehoshaphat didn't let wealth make him arrogant—he prioritized worship, fasting, and prayer during crises. He was a wealthy king who invested in spiritual education and national righteousness. Jehoshaphat remained steady in the things of GOD.

Josiah became king when he was only 8 years old. He was a kid, so he listened to somebody in order to rule properly. He used wealth for restoration of the Temple by overseeing the funding of offerings to rebuild and repair the Temple, (2 Chronicles 34–35). *He* sought God early. And he led a major spiritual reform: tore down idols, restored the Temple, renewed the covenant. Josiah was a righteous king who used wealth to restore worship and national obedience.

In summary, the righteous kings used wealth very well and very wisely. David gave financially of both his own personal and of the national treasure to build a House for God, their beloved Temple.

Jehoshaphat invested in education, and trusted God in battles.

Josiah used wealth to repair the Temple and lead a national repentance.

,Wealth wasn't condemned—it was a tool, for these kings as well it can be for you. Do not fear money; it is a necessary tool to do the work of Him who sent you and to reach destiny. The righteous kings treated wealth as God's provision, not personal entitlement. They gave generously to God's work. They led by example in faith, worship, and justice. And they showed humility when corrected (especially Hezekiah). This reflects back to money highlighting who a person is, not changing it. Character flaws will be exaggerated by money when people are prideful or greedy. Godly traits such as those of the Fruit of the Spirit will be magnified when a person has means to express themselves and their true nature.

The same is true for you. Therefore, consider that if you don't have money or have the amount you believe you should have, absent witchcraft working against you, could it be that God is waiting for you to develop in Fruit of the Spirit, and in character and in soul prosperity?

If witchcraft is working against you, delaying your receiving money and wealth, could it be that God is waiting for you to arise and do warfare so you can rid your life of that evil, so that when God blesses you, you will keep it?

Aren't You A King?

I mention these kings because aren't you a king? Do you think God has or likes broke kings. How can you be a king and be broke? The power to get wealth from Deuteronomy 8:18 is chiefly so God can establish covenant with you. So you shouldn't be broke.

If you don't believe that, do believe that you are a captain of industry, or a king of commerce if you are in the marketplace or in the workforce? Yes, then, Amen.

Are you in Covenant with GOD? Do you know what the contract of your covenant with God says? Are you keeping Covenant?

Wealth should neither be worshipped nor condemned. It is a tool to use. 40% of people are poor. Help them! Money will flow to you because you are a king and in covenant with the King of kings. It is provision from God. Then the money that flows because you are a king (Jesus is King of kings), and you are a royal priesthood should be handled the way kings and priests handle money.

Money:

- It serves you.
- It serves God's purposes.
- It serves God's people.
- It serves God's missions.
- It serves.
- It is used for teaching and evangelism.
- It is not to heap on your own lust.

Yes, you can live in the overflow, of what God provides, but if your heart is not right toward God and you know you will abuse money, then you should fear it. Do you trust yourself? If you cannot trust yourself, then how can God trust you?

But it is wiser to fear God and let Him, by His Spirit show you how to handle and be a conqueror over money. Else, money can be a trap.

Money as Bait

Unconsecrated, undedicated money is very risky to have in your wallet, purse, or bank account. There is no need to fear money when you've identified several things. One is: *What do you want money for?* The second question might be, *Does God agree?*

The devil gives money, as bait to trap folks, initiate them, or mess them up. Walk wisely. To counter this, we acknowledge God in all of our ways and in all of our money.

Free standing money with no purpose or destination to it...is most likely **bait**. (Not always, it could be *miracle money* that you either prayed for, need, or didn't even pray for, but it comes to you by the providence of God. But you need to hurry to consecrate it and dedicate it to God so it can be blessed and you can keep it, enjoy it, and use it for what God intends you to use it for.

Regarding money, any money: Ask God: Is this from You, Lord? If you accept it, consecrate your gain to the Lord. In Genesis, Abel brought his offering to the Lord at the appointed time. Cain? It is said that in the process of time, (Genesis 4:5). Do you know how much devilment could have gotten into Cain's farm, land, crops, livestock, and even Cain *in the process of time*? Cain was operating with no protection really because he hadn't brought his offering to the altar of God as God had instructed.

Money with No assignment needs assignment. And it needs that assignment as soon as possible, not in the *process* or the fullness of time.

It doesn't mean that you have to spend all the money you get, even though the Bible warns of hoarding. In the Bible, the LORD says bring ye the tithes so that there will be meat in mine house, (Malachi 3:10).

Loose money, wild money, uncertain riches is most likely bait or a trap. If it is too good to be true, it usually isn't good or true.

While men slept, the devil sowed tares. **the devil sowed.** Something that is *sowed* is strewn about, versus being placed, strategically and properly placed. If money is just laying about seemingly for the taking, be careful.

The Word says that we are the **planted** of the LORD: We serve a God of order. Planted things are placed in position and watched, nurtured, fed, protected, guarded. Plants, seedlings, saplings are swaddled in soil and then they grow. Careful of "found" money.

Money Is a Magnifier

MONEY IS A MAGNIFIER. Whatever you are, it will be magnified with money and by money--, by virtue of you having money. Good or Bad. Whatever you are, you will be magnified.

Money is a magnifier because money goes on altars. Automatically. It will either go on a Godly altar if you choose to put your money, with intention, in faith there. Or it will automatically go on an evil altar because the evil altar is the default in this Earth.

People who think they are Switzerland, sorry, there is no neutral altar. Atheists, agnostics, where and how you spend your money is accounted for on some altar, somewhere, even if you think you are not spiritual. If you do not choose spirituality, it will be chosen for you, and the default is the dark kingdom or hell. This is binary. There is Heaven and there is hell. After this life there is no neutral place. There is no *nothing* place. Souls and spirits live on; people do not just end in the dirt nap.

Now that the money or whatever you use for increase is on an altar it will magnify because that is what altars do. Altars are busy places they interface the physical with the natural and your "offering" is not the only one on the altar. One can put a thousand to flight and two 10,000. Altars are collective or corporate, whether you realize it or not. Yes, you may have an individual altar in your home, but eventually what you put on that altar joins other altars, just like a stream joins a river and a river joins the ocean. Eventually. Now what you've put on it is magnified because you are saying by your offering being that that you agree with all those people who either knowingly or unknowingly, willingly or unwillingly put their money on that altar as well.

What goes on an altar is magnified because altars don't stop. There is a time component; once an altar gets fired up and started, it will keep on. So, in this magnification, it increases because in time it keeps repeating and repeating, thereby enlarging the situation or magnifying it.

That is, until you make it stop. Until you renounce the offering and denounce it and pull down or destroy the evil altar. It will keep on until you do some spiritual warfare and make it stop.

Money Is a Memory Maker

MONEY IS A MEMORY MAKER. All kinds of people came to Jesus, rich and poor. For example, the rich young ruler, centurions, Cornelius. Cornelius your offerings have come up as a memorial to Me.

And Cornelius said, Four days ago I was fasting until this hour; and at the ninth hour I prayed in my house, and, behold, a man stood before me in bright clothing, And said, Cornelius, thy prayer is heard, and thine alms are had in remembrance in the sight of God. (Acts 10:30-31)

When you get money from God, it should cause you to **REMEMBER GOD**.

But remember the Lord your God, for it is he who gives you the ability to produce wealth, and so confirms his covenant, which he swore to your ancestors, as it is today. (Deuteronomy 8:18).

When God gets money from you, it causes Him to **REMEMBER YOU**, as Cornelius was remembered in the verse above from the Book of Acts.

Those people who are feeling lost, alone, forgotten, when God gets money from you, it causes God to remember you. Your gift will make room for you. Every time you look at the plant that your neighbor gave you, doesn't it bring a sweet thought to your mind? Every time you wear the sweater your daughter gave you for your birthday, don't you remember them? It is built in. Money, that is gifts are memory makers.

You esteem God lightly; He will operate in that same "energy" and esteem you lightly as well. People are like that, too. You give somebody something when you want something from them, they will know. But if you are a consistent, regular giver, that carries far more weight than if you just give every now and then.

Cornelius is praying and asking God for something and the angel showed up and said, Cornelius your prayer is heard because of your gifts and alms that you have given. So, your own daughter calls you and says, Mom, I really want a chocolate cake, would you make one for me? And the answer is certainly yes. But the sour child who doesn't call, doesn't visit, didn't even remember your birthday, you as a human might not even pick their call. Money and gifts are like Post-it notes, they are little reminders that this person either loves me or is at least thinking of me. It's why friends do little nice things for one another from time to time. It's why couples give, it is because they love.

God first loves us, but when we give to God it is making God know that we really do love Him.

Conquer Money

We need wealth to establish covenant with God, so says the Word.

We need money because we have to prove to God that we know what we are doing with money. We need money to live and function. For all these reasons and more, each of us must <u>conquer</u> money. It is not something that should conquer you, you must conquer it. If you are afraid of money, it has conquered you.

Money is a power. It is the lowest power on Earth. Yet it could be a huge stumbling block for many people who don't want to face it, look at it, or handle it. or be responsible for it in any way.

You conquer it by doing things with money and steward over it as you should.

That's probably why Jesus taught so much on it – approximately 1/3 of His teachings, so, we could learn how to conquer it. If you don't conquer money, how will you conquer anything else, if money is the lowest power on Earth? How will you step up and conquer the next power?

Money could be easy to conquer or not easy to conquer because it is a Power. It has power. Therefore, you need more power than money to conquer money. This is why we need God. He is far more powerful than Mammon. When you give offerings, you unseat Mammon off of the throne of your heart and the LORD God takes that position which is where He should be which is a form of deliverance.

The power of God was certainly proved in the Old Testament when the statue to Dagon was found knocked over and lying on the floor every morning, next to the Ark of the Covenant. God is Almighty, He is Omnipotent. Amen. You can play around with money and Mammon all you want, but until you call in Jehovah God, you will not overcome the dark anointing that is on evil money from the dark kingdom.

What does that dark anointing do? When you use that money, it can initiate you into whatever group that it came from. When you use the things or services of a group, you are now a part of them and you now owe them. Dark money can be the beginning of the oppression or possession of a person We need God behind our money to fight the dark money that is on evil altars. This is why we put money purposefully, willingly, knowingly on Godly altars.

A human doesn't fight an altar. Altars fight altars.

Money has anointing. Is the anointing on money good or bad? Depends. Has it been dedicated? And to what? Has it been consecrated? You have the power and responsibility to consecrate money--, your money. Consecrated money will do Godly things for you and others.

Unconsecrated Money

Unconsecrated money can be captured. Money in your possession that has not been dedicated is easy for the devil to steal.

Consecrated money can do more things for you. it will last longer. It will protect you, you will enjoy it. In that consecration is the power to enjoy your wealth, as well as the power to get more wealth. God gives us the power to get wealth. When the prophet told the widow woman to 'make me a cake first", note that **first** means she was consecrating that meal and that oil. Consecrated money, consecrated things don't wear out, they last. As I said before on the altar, they multiply, and they don't run out. When something gets on a spiritual altar it lives.

Without faith it is impossible to please God. So, on the **promise** you consecrate the gift, the blessing, the wealth, the money. One reason is so it will not be captured.

Unconsecrated money can be captured or stolen from you. God protects consecrated money, you know from the guy that wants to steal, kill, and destroy. So without faith it is impossible to please God, so at the whisper, the slightest hint that God is going to bless you financially or some other way, at the promise, go ahead and consecrate the gift. By faith, do it now, the sooner the better, because by faith we are already touching the promise of God, Amen. If for no other reason, it's so it will not be captured, and you will actually receive it.

Let's say money is ABC's. You learn those in kindergarten. If you never learn ABC's you can't build words and you may not be able to leave kindergarten. Money is a basic power that we all must learn how to handle here on Earth because of all the other things we can build with it.

Sometimes we make money into way more than it is. It can be worshipped. Money knows how people feel about it so a *god* named Mammon has associated or inserted itself into money so it can get worship from those who are desperate for, lust for, and/or worship money.

The Fear of Losing Money

The fear of losing money, whether your own or someone else's, is very real. As we know the Lord has not given us a *spirit of fear*, but there is a very real Thief that roams about seeking to devour. He has workers such as emptiers, swallowers, devourers, and destroyers working for him to steal from people. Saved or unsaved, there are thieves out and about in the spirit and in the natural. We hide things, we lock things away, we give things to banks and other places for safekeeping, but the devil seems to have also gone digital, and he devises ways to steal all the time. From phishing to hacking and demanding online and bitcoin ransoms, things can be lost or stolen.

So, by losing I'm not just talking about dropping something from your pocket that has a hole in it. But still, spiritually it is as though the enemy can rip a hole in a pocket that had no hole and have a person asking, where did that go? I know I had it here. Saints of God, if you lose things that you know were in your possession, especially money and financial instruments, go for deliverance. You may need deep deliverance by that time.

The devil has devised many ways to steal from people, therefore you need to be wise and also prayed up. Holes in pockets. Holes in hands, siphoning or draining tubes, these are all spiritual demonic technologies to steal from people. Trauma, sudden losses and sudden repairs that are needed, new car, new refrigerator, washer and dryer that you had not planned or budgeted to buy. These are all forms of the devil stealing from you. Oh, don't argue that you now have a new car so you didn't lose anything. Oh really? Now you didn't get to pay your kid's tuition, so they have to sit out for a semester. Education was stolen, time was stolen and money on the other end was stolen because when your kid finished college they could have had a job that paid actual money, but now they are a semester behind and someone else got that good paying job. That theft could have caused a cascade of negative events. It is best to stay on God's timeline for your life and not devolve into the devil's evil, satanic, or witchcraft timeline.

The washer and dryer money you were planning to invest in something that would have paid you dividends in a few years to enhance your retirement portfolio. The point is the devil should have no place in deciding what you buy or when. He should have no standing in dictating when you make a purchase of durable items for your home, or when or if you can go on vacation or buy new clothes. If he is in your money at all, even if the choices you are having to make don't look like losses, they are. I say that because the devil didn't come here for you to have life and have it more abundantly--, Jesus did. Jesus should be the only person in your finances and in your money and in your life, period.

So, consecrate your gain to the Lord, soonest.

Arise and thresh, O daughter of Zion: for I will make thine horn iron, and I will make thy hoofs brass: and thou shalt beat in pieces many people: and I will consecrate their gain unto the Lord, and their substance unto the Lord of the whole earth. (Micah 4:13)

OPM – Other People's Money

The ramification of losing someone else's money is probably the biggest fear that people who fear money have. And they should worry about that. The Bible says we are to be faithful in another man's things. That means if we work for that man or run errands for that man, or whatever we do for him we should be steadfast in it. Especially when what we touch of another person's involves money, we must be diligent, else, the cost for missteps or mistakes may fall onto us.

Most of all nobody wants to be accused of anything such as stealing, and most of all nobody wants to be accused of stealing someone else's money. Neither does anyone want to be blamed for money fiascos.

Bless Your Food, Bless Your Money

Some love food, some love wine, there is a *god* for all of that. Alcohol is a *spirit*; money is a **power**. Food? There is a *god* for that as well that is another reason why we consecrate and bless food before we use it, don't we? Don't we bless our food before we eat it. We wash our clothes when we buy them new in the store don't we, before we wear them? Well, I do. I wash sheets, towels, all that. We don't know where all that has been or who touched it. Some go so far as to anoint everything they bring into their house and intend to use, especially on their bodies before they use or wear any of those things. There are some things that cannot be consecrated or dedicated for use. Only the Lord can advise you of what should be destroyed and never used in your home or on your person. For example, we are not to eat food dedicated to idols. If we are not to eat it, then it stands to reason that the evil dedication on food cannot be undone? We have to ask the Lord in every case.

What about our money? What about the money that bought that stuff? Then shall we not dedicate and consecrate money before use?

More Than a Conqueror

If money is the lowest power on Earth, if a person never conquers it, what of the other powers that we are to conquer?

The miracles the Jesus performed show that whatever you are looking for Jesus has got all that. Food. Money. Healing. Shall you say to the Lord, I'll take the food, and the healing, but leave the other? We are redeemed from sickness, poverty & death. It's a package deal.

God's got all that. So, if you are giving something to God, you are not giving Him something that **He** needs, you are putting in His hands something that **<u>you</u> need consecrated**. Let it be done on Earth, as it is in Heaven.

If He can send people out on a boat to catch more fish than they've ever caught, giving to God is not for God, it's for you. Jesus has it all, food, money, blessings, healing, success. We are called to be wise stewards so we must not fear that we are called to steward over.

(And this author believes that we cannot opt out of stewardship because we just don't want to do it.)

Evil Dedicated Money

Before wrapping up this book, I want to talk about dangerous money: the worst is money that has been dedicated to the dark kingdom, and it is being presented to you as an opportunity. The enemy wants you to take the temptation and put that in your hands, in your wallet, or your bank account or retirement fund. Crooked money, dark money, stolen money, evil money— money that has already been dedicated to evil, like food that has been dedicated to evil, you don't eat that. So, if money has been dedicated to the dark where is that money from? Is it, like food that has been dedicated to idols, is this money dedicated already? Don't accept it.

Loan sharks and the like that is the money they have. Often, I get calls from people that I say want to "sell me money". You may as well, all those offers you get in the mail and by spam calls and what not. I say sell me money because to get $100. Will cost way more than $100 and sometimes way more than that. This is bait. I hate interest. I hate added fees. I hate usury, yet dark money is all about the trap. Selling you something that God will give you for free.

God will give you money if you do what you are supposed to be doing, and He gives you the fruit of your labor. Money is that fruit.

But the thief will add interest. The blessings of the Lord maketh rich and he adds no sorrow. Interest to me, is sorrow. Especially high interest. Thy are trying to sell something that God will give you if you are consecrating your gain to the Lord.

Could it be that Elisha didn't accept the money from Namaan because of Namaan? Who is the money you are about to receive coming from? You'd better know. It won't have a stamp on it that says, "dark money". George Washinton's face will not be replaced with an image of Lucifer, so you have to know by discernment.

Accepting it will make an alliance with whom? Spiritually? What kingdom? Depends on where it is coming from.

Naaman was healed from leprosy, the prophet did not accept Naaman's offering, but Gehazi did and Gehazi got leprosy. Every dollar ain't' a good dollar, especially if it will make you to become LIKE the person that gave it to you, "lent" it to you, or sold it to you, or LIKE the *god* they serve.

Fruit- Lump, Root-Branch

Ask the Lord, if I put my hands on this money, LORD, can it be consecrated to the LORD?

The next most dangerous money is unconsecrated money: this money is spiritually up for grabs. If the root is holy the lump is holy. Whatever you do with the first of that money, first fruits or first 10 percent declares to all of the spiritual world who you have dedicated the money to. That is the altar that you are putting the first portion of that money on. Is it an evil altar, or a Godly altar? You need to know and you need to be intentional.

For if the firstfruit be holy, the lump is also holy: and if the root be holy, so are the branches. (Romans 11:16)

Whatever your spiritual root is like, or whatever is the spiritual root of the source of that money in that foundation—is it evil or godly, that tells you what kind of money that is. And wherever you put the first fruits or the tithe, or the offering—the first or the best of it, is tells the spirit world who you are serving and how you are consecrating that money.

If you are not consecrating it to God then He can't protect you or it. God has given Earth to man. God need permission to be involved in your life and in your money. Give God permission so He can protect you, and keep you and provide for you. He cannot make it last like the oil and meal lasted for the widow woman if He is not invited to be *in* it, or involved in it. He cannot keep you in provision if you are not consecrating it to Him and you are breaking covenant.

Who you consecrate this money to is automatic in the sense that it is automatically the devil and his kingdom if you don't take the steps to consecrate your gain to the LORD.

Saints of God, this teaching is the Lord's doing, the Holy Spirit is teaching this. It has levels and layers.

Money is bait. Wild money, unconsecrated money, just laying around like cheese in a mousetrap Sitting in traps. Pits. Snares. Covens. Occultic groups.... When the dark kingdom promises power doesn't that include money? Doesn't it most often start with money? Isn't that why people go there? It's why the devil needs money, for the people who come there looking for it. The deal won't go as they expect, but still people don't ask God, but they go to dark and dangerous places. In those places that is where they will find dark and dangerous money.

We can't also go there by letting our money go there. We do that by doing the wrong thing or doing nothing. You decide like Jehoshaphat, you are going to consecrate the money to yourself. I've told you there is anointing on money and without God you are no match for the devil. When you heap on your own lust. Saints of God, when you are backed in a corner and you heap that money on your own bills because they are desperately due, leaving God out, then God is just out and you are on your own.

Lord Jesus, help us all.

Nobody asked Jesus for money but for some reason they ask the devil for money? Why is that? dark MONEY. Yes, be aware of it. Based on the root. Where did it come from. Be afraid of it, but have a righteous fear knowing that you can walk away from it or take authority over it, if the Lord says the same.

Pray for discernment to know the difference between Godly money and trap money. Do not destroy your destiny by taking what God is not giving you

You must conquer money. Know that in Christ you can walk away from dark money and not be tempted. You can take authority over evil money because the greater one is in us. Go to where the Lord makes rich and adds no sorrow, in the Name of Jesus.

People of God, do not sabotage yourself, your purpose, your ministry, your destiny by taking from the hand that is not God's hand. Do not take what God is not giving you.

And do not risk your destiny by rejecting what God is trying to give you. You were not made for fear and fear should not rule you, nor any other idol god or evil spirit. Do not let the enemy put so many evil influences in you or around you that you become afraid of things that you should have dominion and authority of. You are more than a conqueror in Christ Jesus.

.Do not fear money, receive that righteous money from God and be sure to consecrate it back to Him. The blessings of the LORD maketh rich and He adds no sorrow with it.

Consecrate your gain to the Lord. To protect it, to extend it--, even in times of famine. To multiply it, like huge loads of fish in a net that won't break. To keep it, to enjoy it and be able to pass it down to your generations. When you dedicate and consecrate your money to the Lord, you indicate what GOD you are serving. Do it every time, with every gain.

Declarations & Prayers

1. Lord, have Mercy on me, a sinner. If I am none of Yours give me a Godly sorrow and a repentant heart for my sins and make me one of Yours.
2. I believe that Jesus is the Son of God and that He came to Earth, and was crucified, and on the third day, God resurrected Him, and He lives.
3. I believe with my heart and I confess with my mouth that Jesus is Lord and I am saved, Thank You, Lord.
4. Lord, fill me with Your Spirit, Your Holy Spirit to empower me in my life and these prayers, in the Name of Jesus.
5. Lord, rebuke the *spirit of fear* from my life in any and all of its forms, in the Name of Jesus, for You have not

given us a *spirit of fear,* but one of love, power, and a sound mind and boldness in the Name of Jesus.

6. I am not afraid, for the Lord is with me always. I am not afraid of money. I am not afraid to receive money, but I receive it, I use it well and wisely to the praise of God's glory, in the Name of Jesus.

7. I rebuke every *spirit of slavery* that requires me to make do or suffer without, in the Name of Jesus.

8. Jesus came that I might have life and have it more abundantly, in the Name of Jesus.

9. I rebuke the *spirit of complacency*, or just enough, in the Name of Jesus.

10. C-level, average and mediocrity, I rebuke you, in the Name of Jesus. My life should be one of excellence to glorify God, in the Name of Jesus.

11. I am the righteousness of God in Christ Jesus; I do not think more of myself than I ought, but I do not

think less of myself than God says that I should, in Jesus' Name.

12. I am a *little k* king in the Earth, I am a royal priesthood forever after the order of Melchizedek, and I will stand, work, and walk with dignity and honor in my respective offices forever, to the glory of God, in Jesus' Name, Amen.

    a. Thank You Lord.

13. I will esteem the Lord to the Highest because He is the Great God and I will acknowledge Him in all I do, Amen.

14. I let my praises and gifts and offerings flow freely to the God of my Covenant, Jehovah, Amen.

15. In the Name of Jesus and by the discernment of the Holy Spirit, I shun problem money, dark money, evil money, evil dedicated money, trick money, trap money, and any funds that I should not touch, hold, use, or handle, in the Name of Jesus.

16. Money that comes to me shall be consecrated to the Lord. All my gain will be consecrated to the Kingdom of Light, in the Name of Jesus.

17. I do not fear money; it serves me. It serves people. It serves God's plan for this world, in the Name of Jesus.

18. I do not fear math or numbers or large quantities of money for I walk in the Wisdom of God, in the Name of Jesus.

19. I do not lust for money; money is my servant, in the Name of Jesus.

20. I do not serve Mammon; I only serve Jehovah God, in the Name of Jesus.

21. I pursue purpose, destiny, and spiritual things; I do not chase money. I pursue Wisdom and with Wisdom is wealth in the Name of Jesus.

22. Lord God, erase every bad taste and every evil memory of money or bad things that happened with money or

because of money in my life, in the Name of Jesus.

23. I cast down every evil imagination and memory against my having the wealth that God says I should have, hold, and handle in this life, in the Name of Jesus.

24. Wisdom of God, do not let me be tricked, manipulated, or fooled by the thief or any of his agents that come only to steal, kill, and destroy, in the Name of Jesus.

25. Anointing to receive, use, have, enjoy, handle money come upon me now, in the Name of Jesus

26. Lord, seal up every spiritual hole in my hand and in my pockets, wallets and bank accounts, in the Name of Jesus.

27. Father, remove every spiritual siphoning drain on my finances, in the Name of Jesus.

28. Lord, wash me thoroughly by the washing by the Water of the Word,

and renew my mind that I have the mind of Christ when it comes to understanding, handling, having, receiving money and wealth, in the Name of Jesus.

29. I rebuke and crush any demonic programming in my mind or soul regarding money, in the Name of Jesus.

30. Lord, let me show my moderation when it comes to money, wealth and abundance that I neither shun it, nor lust for it, but I moderate myself, in a way that brings glory to Your Name, in the Name of Jesus.

31. Father, stop me from giving away things that I should keep, in the Name of Jesus.

32. Father, help me to give away things that I should not hold on to, in the Name of Jesus.

33. Lord, help me to give away things properly in a spiritually correct way, and give me Wisdom to know when

I should destroy things rather than give them away at all, in the Name of Jesus.

34. Father by discernment and Wisdom, stop me from giving to any ungodly altar, whether it be a physical altar, a moving altar, such as a person, or an unseen spiritual altar, in the Name of Jesus.

35. Lord, give me Wisdom, discernment and courage not to renew evil covenants on money altars, even if it is a family altar, in the Name of Jesus.

36. I break a *people-pleasing spirit* off of me now, in the Name of Jesus. I please God; only God, in the Name of Jesus.

37. As a vessel of blessing, Lord let me receive the givers spirit and give appropriately when moved to by the Spirit of God, in the Name of Jesus.

38. Lord, bridle my tongue, help me guard my mouth that I am not

braggadocious and that I do not tell more than I should of any financial matters of my life, in the Name of Jesus.

39. I break free of users and takers and moochers, in the Name of Jesus.

40. Thank You, Lord, by Jesus Christ's work at Calvary and the Better Covenant I am redeemed from the Curse of the Law. I am redeemed from sickness, death and poverty, in the Name of Jesus.

41. Lord, thank You that You are Lord of the Harvest and You are present to give me abundance in the work of my hands, in the Name of Jesus.

42. Lord, thank You that You give me the fruit of my labor, always, and in abundance, in the Name of Jesus.

43. I dedicate and consecrate my gain to the Lord of Lords, in the Name of Jesus.

44. Lord, increase my anointing in discernment regarding money,

finances and wealth, in the Name of Jesus.

45. Father, thank You that according to Your Word, You give us the power to get wealth so that You may establish covenant with us, in the Name of Jesus.

46. Lord, establish covenant with me, in the Name of Jesus.

47. Lord, let me always remember You, in the Name of Jesus.

48. Father, thank You that You give us power to enjoy our wealth and to eat of it, in the Name of Jesus.

49. Thank You, Lord, for being able to discern trick money, trap money and money intended to initiate into evil and that I am empowered to walk away from it, in the Name of Jesus.

50. Lord, give me the spiritual solution to every problem that I have, especially issues involving money, so that I can break free, break through, receive abundance that

Jesus came that I have, as well as keep wealth that wealth will always be in my house, in the Name of Jesus.

51. **Lord, let Godly wealth and abundance always be in my house, in the Name of Jesus.**

52. I rebuke every *spirit of poverty* from my father's house, my mother's house--, Lord let Godly wealth always be in my house, in the Name of Jesus.

53. Father, now that the enemy who has been stealing from me has been found out, spoil that enemy's house and return to me seven-fold everything that has been stolen from me, in the Name of Jesus.

54. I seal these words, declarations across every realm, dimension, age, timeline, past, present and future to infinity . I seal them with the Blood of Jesus and the Holy Spirit of Promise.

55. Any retaliation against any person speaking, hearing or praying these words and prayers, backfire against the perpetrator to infinity, without Mercy, in the Name of Jesus.

AMEN.

The LORD *is* my light and my salvation; whom shall I fear? the LORD *is* the strength of my life; of whom shall I be afraid? (Psalm 27:1)

Dear Reader:

Thank you for acquiring and reading this book. I pray it will help deliver you from the fear of money and into receiving all that God has for you for life, ministry, purpose, and destiny,

In the Name of Jesus,

Amen.

Dr. Marlene Miles

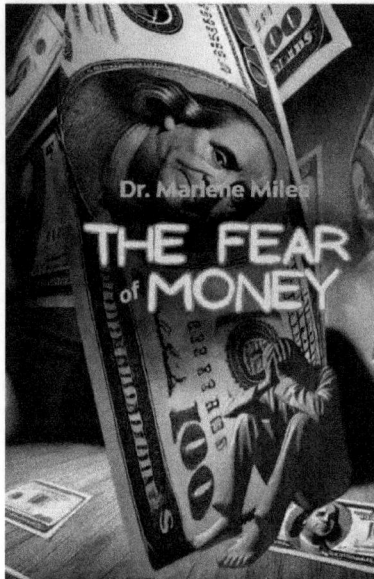

Prayerbooks by this author

While most books by this author have prayer points either throughout the book or at the end, there are some books that are only prayers. You just open up the book and pray.

Prayers Against Barrenness: *For Success in Business and Life*

Fruit of the Womb: *Prayers Against Barrenness*

Beauty Curses, *Warfare Prayers Against* https://a.co/d/5Xlc20M

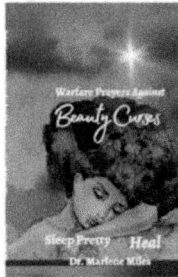

Courts of Marriage: Prayers for Marriage in the Courts of Heaven *(prayerbook)* https://a.co/d/cNAdgAq

Courtroom Warfare @ Midnight
(prayerbook) https://a.co/d/5fc7Qdp

Demonic Cobwebs *(prayerbook)*
https://a.co/d/fp9Oa2H

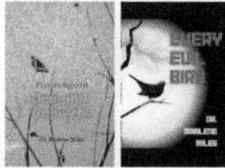

Every Evil Bird https://a.co/d/hF1kh1O

Gates of Thanksgiving

Spirits of Death, Hell & the Grave, Pass Over Me and My House

Throne of Grace: Courtroom Prayer

Warfare Prayer Against Poverty
https://a.co/d/bZ611Yu

Other books by this author

AK: The Adventures of the Agape Kid

Already Married in the Spirit: *Why You May Not Be Married in the Natural*

AMONG SOME THIEVES
https://a.co/d/dkYT4ZV

Ancestral Powers

Anti-Marriage, *The Spirit of*

Backstabbers https://a.co/d/gi8iBxf

Barrenness, *Prayers Against*
https://a.co/d/feUltIs

Battlefield of Marriage, *The*

Beware of the Dog: Prayers Against Dogs in the Dream.

Bless Your Food: *Let the Dining Table be Undefiled*

Blindsided: *Has the Old Man Bewitched You?* https://a.co/d/5O2fLLR

Break Free from Collective Captivity

Broken Spirits & Dry Bones

By Means of a Whorish Father

Casting Down Imaginations

Churchzilla, The Wanna-Be,
Supposed-to-be Bride of Christ

Demonic Cobwebs (prayerbook)

Demonic Time Bombs

Demons Hate Questions

Devil Loves Trauma, *The*

Devil Weapons: Unforgiveness,
Bitterness,...

The Devourers: Thieves of Darkness 2

Do Not Swear by the Moon

Don't Refuse Me, Lord (4 book series)
https://a.co/d/idP34LG

Dream Defilement

The Emptiers: *Thieves of Darkness, 1*
https://a.co/d/5I4n5mc

Evil Touch

Failed Assignment

Fantasy Spirit Spouse
https://a.co/d/hW7oYbX

FAT Demons (The): *Breaking Demonic Curses* https://a.co/d/4kP8wV1

Fear of Money, The

The Fold (5-book series)

- The Fold (Book 1)
- Name Your Seed (Book 2)
- The Poor Attitudes of Money (3)
- Do Not Orphan Your Seed (4)
- For the Sake of the Gospel (5)
- My Sowing Journal

Gang Ups: Touch Not God's Anointed

Getting Rid of Evil Spiritual Food

https://a.co/d/i2L3WYQ

got HEALING? Verses for Life

got LOVE? Verses for Life

got HOPE? Verses for Life

got money? https://a.co/d/g2av41N

Here Come the Horns: *Skilled to Destroy*
https://a.co/d/cZiNnkP

Hidden Sins: Hidden Iniquity

https://a.co/d/4MthOwa

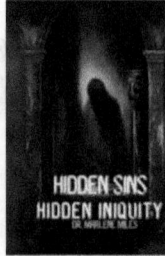

How to Dental Assist

How to Dental Assist2: Be Productive, Not Wasteful

How to STOP Being a Blind Witch or Warlock

I Take It Back

Legacy

Let Me Have A Dollar's Worth
https://a.co/d/h8F8XgE

Level the Playing Field

Living for the NOW of God

Lose My Location
https://a.co/d/crD6mV9

Love Breaks Your Heart

Made Perfect In Love

Mammon https://a.co/d/29yhMG7

Man Safari, *The*

Marriage Ed. Rules of Engagement & Marriage

Made Perfect in Love

Money Hunters: Beware of Those

Money on the Altar https://a.co/d/4EqJ2Nr

Mulberry Tree, *The*
https://a.co/d/9nR9rRb

Motherboard (The)- *Soul Prosperity Series*

Name Your Seed

Occupy: *Until I Return*
https://a.co/d/bZ7ztUy

Plantation Souls

Players Gonna Play

<u>Portals</u>: Shut the Front Door: Prayers to Close Evil Portals.

Power Money: Nine Times the Tithe

https://a.co/d/gRt41gy

The Power to Get Wealth
https://a.co/d/e4ub4Ov

Powers Above

The Robe, Part 1, The Lessons of Joseph

The Robe, Part II, The Lessons of Joseph

Seasons of Grief

Seasons of Waiting

Seasons of War

Second Marriage, Third--, *Any Marriage*

https://a.co/d/6m6GN4N

Seducing Spirits: Idolatry & Whoredoms

https://a.co/d/4Jq4WEs

Shut the Front Door: *Prayers to Close Portals* https://a.co/d/cH4TWJj

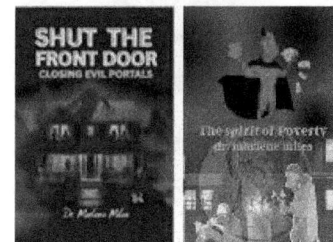

Sift You Like Wheat

Six Men Short: What Has Happened to all the Men?

Soul Prosperity soul prosperity series 3

https://a.co/d/5p8YvCN

Souls Captivity soul prosperity series 2

The Spirit of Anti-Marriage

The Spirit of Poverty
https://a.co/d/abV2o2e

Spiritual Thieves
https://a.co/d/eqPPz33

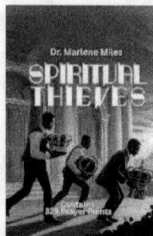

StarStruck- Triangular Power series.

SUNBLOCK- Triangular Power series.

The Swallowers: *Thieves of Darkness*, 3

Take It Back

This Is NOT That: How to Keep Demons from Coming at You

Time Is of the Essence

Too Many Wives: *Why You Have Lady Problems*

Tormenting Spirits
https://a.co/d/dAogEJf

Toxic Souls

Triangular Power *(series)*

- Powers Above
- SUNBLOCK

- Do Not Swear by the Moon
- STARSTRUCK

Unbreak My Heart: *Don't Let Me Die*

Uncontested Doom

Unguarded Hours, *The*

Unseen Life, *The* (forthcoming)

Upgrade: How to Get Out of Survival Mode

- Toxic Souls (Book 2 of series)
- Legacy (Book 3 of series)

The Wasters: *Thieves of Darkness*, Bk 2
https://a.co/d/bUvI9Jo

What Have You to Declare? What Do You Have With You from Where You've Been?

When I Was A Child, *I Prayed As a Child*

When the Devourer is Rebuked

https://a.co/d/1HVv8oq

The Wilderness Romance *(series)* This series is about conducting a Godly relationship and marriage with someone who is a Wilderness person. It is about how to recognize it and navigate through it. These books are about how not to get caught up in such.

- *The Social Wilderness*
- *The Sexual Wilderness*
- *The Spiritual Wilderness*

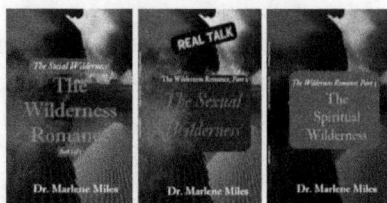

Other Series

The Fold (a series on Godly finances)
https://a.co/d/4hz3unj

Soul   Prosperity   Series
https://a.co/d/bz2M42q

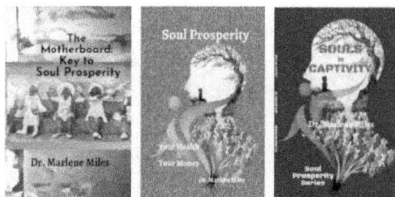

Spirit Spouse books

https://a.co/d/9VehDSo

https://a.co/d/97sKOwm

Battlefield of Marriage, The

https://a.co/d/eUDzizO

Players Gonna Play

https://a.co/d/2hzGw3N

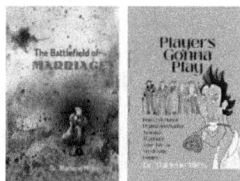

Sent Spirit Spouse (can someone send you a spirit spouse? This book is not yet released.)

Matters of the Heart

Made Perfect in Love
https://a.co/d/70MQW3O

Love Breaks Your Heart
https://a.co/d/4KvuQLZ

Unbreak My Heart
https://a.co/d/84ceZ6M

Broken Spirits & Dry Bones
https://a.co/d/e6iedNP

Thieves of Darkness series

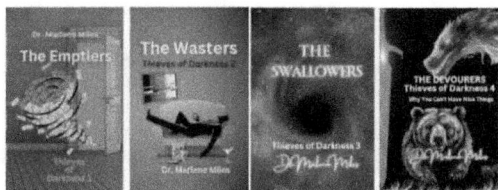

The Emptiers https://a.co/d/heio0dO

The Wasters https://a.co/d/5TG1iNQ

The Swallowers
https://a.co/d/1jWhM6G

The Devourers: Why We Can't Have Nice
Things https://a.co/d/87Tejbf

Spiritual Thieves

Triangular Powers https://a.co/d/aUCjAWC

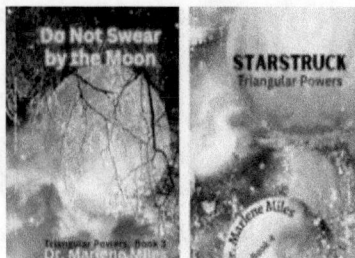

Upgrade (series) *How to Get Out of Survival Mode* https://a.co/d/aTERhXO

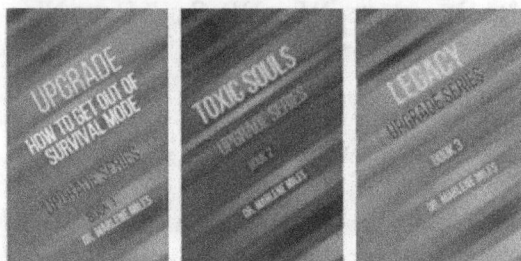

www.ingramcontent.com/pod-product-compliance
Lightning Source LLC
LaVergne TN
LVHW051417080426
835508LV00022B/3129